For Cathy and Marv, with
a great big "bear" hug
—M.B.

Special thanks to Laurie Roulston
of the Denver Museum of Natural History
for her expertise

Photography credits:
Cover: Johnny Johnson/Stone; pages 1–2: Erwin & Peggy Bauer; page 3: Bill Lea/DPA; page 5: Johnny Johnson/Stone; page 6: Claudia Adams/DPA; page 7: Stephen J. Krasemann/Photo Researchers; page 8: Tom McHugh/Photo Researchers; page 9: Zig Leszczynski/Animals Animals; page 10: Gijsbert van Frankenhuyzen/DPA; page 11: Erwin & Peggy Bauer; page 12: Russ Gutshall/DPA; page 13: Rod Planck/DPA; pages 14–15: Erwin & Peggy Bauer; page 17: Kevin Schaefer/Stone; page 18: Jeanne Drake/Stone; page 19 © Yva Momatiuk & John Eastcott/Photo Researchers; pages 20–22: Lynn & Donna Rogers; page 23: Michael Giannechini,/Photo Researchers; page 25: Russ Gutshall/DPA; page 26: Doug Locke/DPA; page 27: Leonard Lee Rue III/Stone; pages 28–30: Lynn & Donna Rogers; page 31: Erwin & Peggy Bauer; page 32: Bruce M. Herman/Photo Researchers; page 33: Bill Lea/DPA; page 35: Erwin & Peggy Bauer; page 36: Fritz Polking/DPA; page 37: Erwin & Peggy Bauer; page 38: Lynn & Donna Rogers.

Growl! A Book About Bears, by Melvin Berger. Copyright © 1999 by Melvin Berger. Reprinted by permission of Scholastic, Inc.

Houghton Mifflin Edition, 2005

Printed in the U.S.A.

ISBN: 0-618-06225-4

12 13 14 B 08 07 06 05 04

GROWL!

A Book About Bears

by Melvin Berger

Hello Reader! Science — Level 3

 HOUGHTON MIFFLIN   BOSTON • MORRIS PLAINS, NJ

California   •   Colorado   •   Georgia   •   Illinois   •   New Jersey   •   Texas

CHAPTER ONE

What Do Bears Eat?

In *Goldilocks and the Three Bears*, the bears eat porridge.
But real bears eat much more than that.
And they're hungry all the time!

There are different kinds of bears.
Each kind has its own diet.

The **grizzly bear** is one kind of bear.
Grizzly bears feed on
- grass and roots,
- fish they catch in the water,
- small animals that hide under the ground,
- and bigger animals like young deer.

The food adds up.
Each grizzly eats about 35 pounds of
food every day.
It takes you almost two weeks to eat
that much!

Grizzly bears eat a lot because they're
so big.
A grizzly can grow to be longer than
a sofa.
It can weigh as much as 10 grown-ups!

Polar bears eat mostly seals.
Sometimes they hunt walruses.
They also feed on fish and whales that
have died.

Polar bears live where it's very cold.
Eating lots of food helps them
keep warm.
So does a thick layer of fat under
their skin.

Most bears like to eat honey.
But **sun bears** really love the
sweet stuff.
That's why they're sometimes called
honey bears.

Sun bears are the smallest bears.
They're the length of a yardstick.
They weigh about as much as a
fourth grader.
Sun bears spend much of their time
climbing and resting in trees.

Sloth bears hunt ants and termites.
The bears break open the nests.
Then they stick out their long tongue.
SLURP!
They suck up the bugs.
What loud noises the sloth bears make!

The sloth bears move very slowly.
That's how they got their name.
"Sloth" is an old word that means
"slow."

Giant pandas eat mostly bamboo.
Without bamboo, they would starve.

Giant pandas have chubby white bodies
with black marks.
They have six fingers on their front paws.
The extra finger is like a thumb.
It helps them hold the bamboo.

People once thought giant pandas were
big raccoons.
Now most think that pandas are
really bears.

CHAPTER TWO

How Do Bears Find Food?

All bears have a big nose called a snout. Can you guess how this helps them fill their tummies with food?

A large snout gives bears a sharp sense
of smell.
It helps them find food.
Did you know that some bears can sniff
a person from a mile away?
They can smell a dead animal at
12 miles!

Bears will travel far to find something
to eat.
But they don't walk on their toes like
most other animals.
Instead, bears walk with their feet flat
on the ground.
They walk just as you do.

Bears can also stand on two legs.

This makes them much taller.

It helps them get food that is hard

to reach.

And it helps them fight off enemies.

For their size, bears are very fast runners.

A big bear can charge a deer at 40 miles

per hour!

That's faster than a horse can gallop.

Few animals can escape a charging bear.

Except for the panda, bears have five
toes on each paw.
And every toe ends in a long, sharp claw.
The claws always stick out.
Bears use their claws to
- dig for roots,
- climb trees,
- pick fruits and berries,
- and catch other animals.

Bears are powerful animals.
They have huge, hairy heads and
mouths full of big teeth.
The pointed front teeth rip into animals
they eat.
The flat back teeth grind up roots
and plants.

Bears are very big.

Their long, shaggy hair makes them look even bigger.

Yet, bears are mostly gentle.

Except — when a person or animal comes near their young or their food.

Then, watch out!

Bears can get angry very fast.

CHAPTER THREE

How Do Most Bears Get Ready for Winter?

In the fall, most bears eat more than
usual.
Every day they stuff themselves
with food.
They eat so much that they get very fat.

The bears then look for places to spend
the winter.

A bear's winter home is called a den.

A den may be

- a cave,

- a hollow tree,

- a space under a big rock,

- a shelter of twigs,

- or a hole dug in the snow.

Soon the weather turns very cold.

The bears can't find enough to eat.

One day it may start to snow.

The bears head for their dens.

They curl up.

And they fall fast asleep!

All winter long, the bears don't eat
or drink.
They live off the fat in their body.
They snore the days and nights away!

The bears sleep for a long time.
But they wake easily.
A loud noise may startle them awake.

Bears sometimes wake up on warm
winter days.
They crawl out of their dens.
They may walk around for a while.
Then the bears head back to their dens.
Before you can say "good night,"
they're snoring again.

Bears *really* wake up when it's spring.

Then they shuffle out of their dens.

At first, they're very thirsty.

They drink lots of water.

Sometimes they eat snow.

Then they look for food.

They sniff the ground in search of grass
and roots.

Bushes and trees are starting to bloom.

Fish, insects, and animals are easy
to find.

Some other animals also sleep
all winter.

We say they hibernate (HI-ber-nate).

Bats, frogs, and snakes hibernate.

They stay asleep for the whole winter.

They breathe very slowly.

Their hearts beat much slower.

And their temperatures drop way down.

But do bears really hibernate?
Bears sleep lightly and wake easily.
Their breathing and heartbeat slow down
only a little.
And their temperature stays nearly
the same.

Some people say bears hibernate.
Some people say bears just take
a long nap.
What do you think?

CHAPTER FOUR

When Are Baby Bears Born?

Most bear babies are born in the middle
of winter.

The mother gives birth in the den.

She usually has two babies at a time.

They are called cubs.

The cubs are tiny.

Each one looks like a rat without a tail.

It weighs about a pound or so.

That's much less than a human baby.

The cubs are helpless.

Their eyes are closed.

They have no teeth.

They have no fur.

And they can't walk.

The cubs stay in the den for about
two months.
The mother bear snuggles them close
to her.
She keeps her babies toasty warm.
And she feeds them milk from
her body.

The cubs grow bigger and bigger.
In spring, the bears come out of
their dens.
The cubs are bouncy and full of fun.
Bear cubs and their mother play
together.

The mother teaches her cubs to hunt
for food.
She fights off any animal that comes
too close.

A mother black bear teaches her cubs
to climb trees.
The cubs feed on nuts and leaves.
They stay there until she tells them
to come down.

A mother polar bear teaches her cubs
to swim.
She also shows them how to catch fish.
Often she gives the cubs rides on
her back.

A mother sun bear teaches her cubs
to hunt at night.
She helps them make a bed of branches
in a tree.
They sleep there during the day.

All cubs stay close to their mothers
for a long while.
Some stay for several months.
Some stay for a few years.

In time, the cubs can care for themselves.

They find their own food.

They look for mates.

Everything starts all over again.

All spring, summer, and fall, the hungry
bears eat and eat.

When winter comes, they crawl into dens.

They go to sleep.

Of course, they snore.

The mother bears have cubs.

They feed and cuddle their babies.

If bears dream, they dream of spring.

Sweet dreams, big and little bears!